Yu-Sheng Lo
Chien-Tsai Liu

Healthcare-associated Infection Surveillance System

Yu-Sheng Lo
Chien-Tsai Liu

Healthcare-associated Infection Surveillance System

LAP LAMBERT Academic Publishing

Impressum / Imprint

Bibliografische Information der Deutschen Nationalbibliothek: Die Deutsche Nationalbibliothek verzeichnet diese Publikation in der Deutschen Nationalbibliografie; detaillierte bibliografische Daten sind im Internet über http://dnb.d-nb.de abrufbar.

Alle in diesem Buch genannten Marken und Produktnamen unterliegen warenzeichen-, marken- oder patentrechtlichem Schutz bzw. sind Warenzeichen oder eingetragene Warenzeichen der jeweiligen Inhaber. Die Wiedergabe von Marken, Produktnamen, Gebrauchsnamen, Handelsnamen, Warenbezeichnungen u.s.w. in diesem Werk berechtigt auch ohne besondere Kennzeichnung nicht zu der Annahme, dass solche Namen im Sinne der Warenzeichen- und Markenschutzgesetzgebung als frei zu betrachten wären und daher von jedermann benutzt werden dürften.

Bibliographic information published by the Deutsche Nationalbibliothek: The Deutsche Nationalbibliothek lists this publication in the Deutsche Nationalbibliografie; detailed bibliographic data are available in the Internet at http://dnb.d-nb.de.

Any brand names and product names mentioned in this book are subject to trademark, brand or patent protection and are trademarks or registered trademarks of their respective holders. The use of brand names, product names, common names, trade names, product descriptions etc. even without a particular marking in this work is in no way to be construed to mean that such names may be regarded as unrestricted in respect of trademark and brand protection legislation and could thus be used by anyone.

Coverbild / Cover image: www.ingimage.com

Verlag / Publisher:
LAP LAMBERT Academic Publishing
ist ein Imprint der / is a trademark of
OmniScriptum GmbH & Co. KG
Heinrich-Böcking-Str. 6-8, 66121 Saarbrücken, Deutschland / Germany
Email: info@lap-publishing.com

Herstellung: siehe letzte Seite /
Printed at: see last page
ISBN: 978-3-659-40737-6

Zugl. / Approved by: Taipei, Taipei Medical University, Dissertation 2015

Chapter I Introduction

1.1 Introduction

Healthcare-associated infections (HAIs) are infections that patients acquire during the course of receiving treatment for other conditions within a healthcare setting [1]. HAI can result in prolonged hospital stay, long-term disability, increased resistance to antibiotics, a massive additional financial burden for the healthcare system, high costs for patients and their families, medical malpractice crisis between healthcare staffs and patients, and even death [2]. Prevention and reduction of HAIs is the major issue for the worldwide nations and healthcare settings.

HAI surveillance is considered the basis of all effective infection control activities which are recognized to be the first step in the prevention of HAI. It has been suggested that intensive surveillance programs might reduce infection rates [3-6]. In order to reduce the infection risk of hospitalized patients, the infection control professionals (ICPs) should conduct comprehensive HAI surveillance tasks by continuously monitoring patients' clinical signs and symptoms, microbiology cultures reports, fever records (especially for temperature is more than or equal to 38°C), radiology images/reports, antibiotic treatments, physician's diagnosis and judgments, and so on. However, it is time-consuming, labor-intensive, and expensive to implement [7]. Most hospitals cannot afford to conduct such comprehensive surveillance activities, when performed manually.

In recent years, the electronic medical records (EMRs) systems are becoming an increasingly pervasive technology in healthcare settings [7-9]. The EMR systems can speed up patient and clinical information flow, facilitate integration of healthcare data and improve the efficiency and quality of medical services. More and more evidence have already shown that the EMR systems can facilitate better documentation, communication, and integration of healthcare data [7-10]. Therefore, using the EMR systems to support HAI surveillance and control are opportunities for ICPs to minimize time spent on data collection and case finding, and to maximize time spent on manual prevention activities [8].

1.2 Motivation

Computerized clinical information systems or EMR systems are becoming increasingly pervasive technologies in healthcare settings. Utilization of EMRs can increase the work efficiency of ICPs and can reduce manual efforts, particularly in suspected case finding and automated data collection. For suspected case finding, many of the researches proposed detection approaches to increase the overall accuracy by using different combinations of the various EMRs at hand. Therefore, the abilities of hospitals to accurately detect HAIs might depend on the supportability of built EMR systems. Since the EMR systems of a hospital can be newly-built or modified, the detection approaches should be adaptable and automated to incorporate EMRs adopted by hospitals. However, how this will be achieved requires further exploration.

More importantly, those detection approaches can reduce manual efforts in suspected case finding; however, ICPs still spend much time conducting many labor-intensive surveillance tasks, such as HAI-related data collection, truly HAIs identification, clusters or careless healthcare practices investigation, and so on. In order to facilitate the ICPs' work efficacy, the development of an electronic HAI surveillance information system (e-HAISIS) is required for effectively supporting the related HAI surveillance tasks. Accordingly, the e-HAISIS should be like a 'computer assistant' that can integrate the useful HAI-related data from existing or different EMRs of a hospital, monitors a patient's states during his/her hospitalization, reduces paperwork by automating routine and mandatory reporting tasks, and so on. Thus, building a high performance e-HAISIS that integrates the related HAI data, detects the suspected HAI cases more precisely and reduces ICPs' workload, is one of the most urgent and challenging issues.

1.3 Outline of the research

This research was divided into five main subsections. Chapter II describes the associated literature reviews of healthcare-associated infection, surveillance of healthcare-associated infection, and electronic surveillance information systems for HAI. Chapter III describes how to identify the variables that are available in the

EMRs systems of the hospital, creates rules for automatically extracting the variables from the EMRs, and then constructs the HAI detection model for predicting the suspected HAI cases, and finally, evaluates this model using retrospective study to check the sensitivity, specificity, and overall accuracy. Chapter IV describes the development of the integrated HAI surveillance information system based on existing EMRs of a hospital for improving the work efficiency of ICPs. Chapter V presents the discussions of this research. Chapter VI presents the conclusions and suggestions for future research.

Chapter II   Literature Review

2.1   Healthcare-associated infection

HAI is the most common complication or comorbidity of hospitalized patients and may be caused by infectious agents from endogenous or exogenous sources [2]. There must be no evidence that the infection was present or incubating at the time of admission to the acute care setting [11-13]. For patients, HAI not only increases hospital stay or economic burden, but also causes physical/mental suffering, and even death; for medical staffs, it not only adds to workload, but also raises the risk of infection; for healthcare settings, it not only reduces medical resources or turnover rate of wards, but also may lead to medical malpractice crisis.

In the US, the nosocomial infection rate was six percent; for the severe hospitalized patients, it was around twenty percent [14]. When comparing hospitalized patients in ICU wards with non-ICU (general) wards, the nosocomial infection rates of the former was from five to ten times more than that of the latter. In addition, the uses of ventilators, urinary catheters, and intravascular catheters were the main causes for increasing prevalence of HAI, particularly for ICU patients [15].

The US Centers for Disease Control and Prevention (CDC) estimates that approximately 1.7 million HAIs occur in hospitals, and with tens of thousands of lives lost each year [16,17]. According to World Health Organization (WHO) reports, HAIs are major worldwide causes of death and disability [4]. Moreover, there exists substantial financial costs to both patients and healthcare systems [16]. The annual financial losses of HAIs were estimated at approximately € 7 billion in Europe, including direct costs only and reflecting 16 million extra days of hospital stay, and were estimated at around $ 6.5 billion in the US [18].

Since 1988, the US CDC has published guidelines to define HAIs and surveillance criteria for specific types of HAI in acute care settings [11-13]. A more recent version of the CDC's guidelines was published in 2009 and defined thirteen types of HAI [13]. A majority of HAIs include: urinary tract infection (UTI), surgical site infection (SSI), blood stream infection (BSI), and pneumonia (PNEU, which is usually ventilator-associated). The estimated proportion of the four major types of

HAIs in US hospitals was 78%. Of these, there are 36% for UTI, 20% for SSI, 11% for PNEU, and 11% for BSI, respectively [16]. In Taiwan, the estimated proportion of the four major types of HAIs was around 92.5 %. Of these, there are 43.7% for UTI, 10.9% for SSI, 9.8% for PNEU, and 28.1% for BSI, respectively [19]. Accordingly, UTI and BSI are the most common types of HAI and account for approximately 50% or above of all HAIs. In recent years, the US department of Health and Human Services (HHS) declared the reducing of HAIs as an agency priority goal for the department, particularly for BSI and UTI [17]. HAIs are critical patient safety and healthcare quality issues [20]. Studies demonstrated that 10%-70% of HAIs can be preventable [21-23]. Prevention and reduction of HAI has become one of the top priorities for healthcare settings.

2.2 Surveillance of healthcare-associated Infection

HAI surveillance is a systematic, ongoing data collection, analysis and reporting process that quantitatively monitors temporal trends in the occurrence and distribution of susceptibility and resistance to antimicrobial agents, and provides information useful as a guide to medical practice, including therapeutics and disease control activities [24]. For reducing the risk of HAIs, routinely surveillance tasks should be conducted by ICPs. The recommended surveillance methods were proposed, as shown in Table 1 [25].

Table 1 : Surveillance methods and the corresponding descriptions

Surveillance methods	Description
Active vs. Passive	Active : trained personnel use various data sources to identify events
	Passive : non-trained personnel identify and report events to you
Prospective vs. Retrospective	Prospective: monitoring patients while still in the institution; includes post-discharge period for SSI
	Retrospective: case-finding based solely on chart review after patient discharged
Patient-based vs. Laboratory-based	Patient-based: monitoring patients for events, risk factors, and procedures and practices related to patient care
	Laboratory-based: case-finding based solely on positive lab findings
Incidence vs. Prevalence	Incidence: measure new events occurring during some defined time period
	Prevalence: measure all events occurring at either a point in time or during some defined time period
Priority-directed vs. Comprehensive	Priority-directed: objectives for surveillance are defined and focused on specific events and/or patients
	Comprehensive: continuous monitoring of all patients for all events
Risk-adjusted vs. Crude	Risk-adjusted: rates are controlled for variations in the distribution of major risk factors associated with an event's occurrence
	Crude: rates assume equal distribution of risk factors for all events

One of the most effective approaches to prevention and reduction HAIs is comprehensive hospital-wide surveillance that detects changes in clinical signs that require frequent, repeated and detailed bedside assessment on a patient by patient basis [12,13]. This method can detect most suspected HAIs in a population. However, it is time-consuming, labor-intensive, and expensive to implement [7]. For example, according to the case definitions of healthcare-associated UTI (HAUTI) in the 2009 CDC guidelines [13], the ICPs should comprehensively observe the criteria that are related to a patient's signs and symptoms, routine urine tests, urine culture tests, blood culture tests, invasive devices, antibiotic use, physician diagnosis, and clinical and radiographic evidences of infection during the patient's hospitalization. Therefore, the surveillance activities may involve a bedside investigation and the review of medical records such as nursing care charts, treatment charts, laboratory test reports, radiographic exam reports, and medical care records [26]. Consequently, most hospitals with limited resources cannot afford such comprehensively surveillance tasks.

In practice, some hospitals with limited resources have adopted alternative methods which aim to reduce the time required for data collection and case finding [27]. These methods may be termed selective surveillance methods as they aim to select a subset of the population who are likely to have, or develop an infection, just like risks factors for infections, patients with positive culture tests results, patients with a fever and/or prescribed antibiotics, etc [28,29]. Selective surveillance methods are less expensive and time-consuming to implement, compared to comprehensive hospital-wide surveillance of the total population; but these methods can result in incomplete data, a delay in the identification of problems, representativeness of the sample, and difficulty in recognizing clusters of infection [30,31].

HAI surveillance is a challenging task because it requires a particular expertise (usually possessed by ICPs) to assess the quality of the information obtained from infectious data. ICPs can formulate these information into knowledge used for intervention and prevention measures. Moreover, there still are some labor-intensive surveillance tasks that require face-to-face contact with people, such as improving handwashing, performing preventive education and consulting, identifying infection clusters or careless healthcare practices, and studying new invasive devices and technologies that might reduce HAIs. Due to these reasons, ICPs have to compromise between available resources and the quality of infection control. Accordingly, more and more ICPs have adopted e-HAISISs in order to reduce their heavy workload, as some manual surveillance tasks can be automated and replaced [32].

9

2.3 Electronic surveillance information systems for HAI

With increased adoption of EMR systems in recent years [7-9], more and more sophisticated HAI surveillance data are made available in the EMRs. Since the increased HAI-related data can be routinely or automatically collected, the e-HAISISs might be implemented in a cost-effective way. Accordingly, innovative e-HAISISs are being developed for supporting the HAI surveillance and control [33].

A recent systemic review by Bruin defined that electronic data used for HAI surveillance can be classified into three categories: clinical- and laboratory-based data, medico-administrative data, and mixed data [34]. Clinical- and laboratory-based data can refer to a patient's vital signs, biochemistry test results, microbiology culture test results, and radiology reports results. Medico-administrative data can refer to a patient's procedure and discharge codes, prescription records, and physician narratives, but excludes his/her admission and tracking data. Moreover, if electronic data comes from the both categories, it is called mixed-data. In Appendix 1, there presented many e-HAISISs which used different electronic data sources. These e-HAISISs were designed for detecting a variety types of HAI, including SSI and postoperative wound infection (PWIs) [35-50], UTI [26,31,36,40,42,45,51-53], BSI [40,42,31,51,52,54], central venous catheter-related infection (CRI) and central line-associated BSI (CLABSI) [43,31,51,52,54-57], pneumonia and lower respiratory tract infection (RTI) [40,42,43,51,52,58-61], Clostridium difficile infection (CDI) [40,62], and drain-related meningitis [63].

There were some e-HAISISs implemented by using clinical- and laboratory-based data [31,51,53,59,61,67]. Some studies alone relied on microbiology culture test results for identifying the patients with positive culture tests so that a further bedside investigation can be performed [38,41,56,57,64,65]. Some of the studies associated the microbiology culture test results with the biochemistry results, clinical patient data and/or radiology results for detecting the suspected HAI cases by using the defined computer algorithm rules [51,53,59]. Other studies made use of natural language processing systems for detecting hospital-associated pneumonias through extracting infection indications from the free-text radiology reports results [58,61]. Overall, these systems had good sensitivity (range: 60 to 95%) and excellent specificity (range: 83.9 to 100%) for electronic versus conventional surveillance. Moreover, there were two studies that used algorithms based on increases in organism numbers over a baseline to determine alert thresholds for the prediction of nosocomial outbreaks [66,67].

Some e-HAISISs used medico-administrative data [38,44,48,50,68-70]. Through medico-administrative data, there were more than half studies related to SSI. Three studies solely adopted procedure and discharge codes for detecting SSIs. However, there existed quite different sensitivities (80%, 62%, and 20.6%, respectively) [35,37,43]. One study adopted different electronic data sources for detecting Clostridium difficile-related infection; however, the best sensitivity was 80.7% while using only ICD-9-CM codes [62]. Many studies have associated the procedure and discharge codes with pharmacy dispensing records to select the surveillance predictors according to their built statistical models [36,38,47,50,68], and afterwards, they made comparisons between the different detection models [68], or built the e-HAISISs for detecting a variety of SSIs [38,48]. Also, two studies intended to combine procedure and discharge codes and/or pharmacy dispensing records for finding the better detection strategy [44,69,70]. One study for detecting SSIs adopted semiautomated method that was manually verified by infection control experts and can achieve excellent sensitivity (97.8%) and high specificity (91.5%) [46].

Afterwards, there were other e-HAISISs related to mixed-data [26,49,55,60,63,71]. Some studies used two or even more electronic data sources to make comparisons between using individual ones, respectively, or to combine the different electronic data sources to obtain better sensitivity and specificity than when solely using the individual ones, respectively [39,42,45,52,55,60,71]. Accordingly, most systems that adopted the combinations of more than one electronic data source can improve the detection performance [39,42,45,55,60,71]; however, one study indicated that using a single electronic data source can present the best sensitivity (99.3%) with decent specificity (56.8%) [52]. Moreover, there were two studies that used the different electronic variables for building the detection model; the resulting predictive models yielded excellent sensitivity (100% and 98.8%) and specificity

(87.9% and 94.61%) [26,63] .

These publications provide good background while using the various electronic HAI-related data sources for supporting HAI surveillance and control, particularly in suspected case finding. Many electronic detection approaches, which adopted the different combinations of the different electronic data (variables), set a goal of increasing overall accuracy. Accordingly, in previous literature reviews, most electronic detection approaches resulted in better sensitivity and specificity. However, since the case definitions in the CDC's guidelines for HAI surveillance are the most detailed and comprehensive, the different types of HAI were associated with different sets of variables. It also implied that the electronic detection approaches can not adopt a fixed set of electronic variables for detecting all types of HAI, but rather a more flexible set, adapted and automated to deal with the increased electronic data sources of hospitals.

Although most literatures indicated that using electronic detection approaches can reduce time and manual efforts in suspected case finding, ICPs still spend the most time on data collection, medical chart reviews, bedside investigation, and data translation into knowledge for determining cases that are truly HAIs. As a few studies have demonstrated, when ICPs can easily access the related HAI data such as a patient's profile, microbiology laboratory results, antibiotics treatments, and so on, the work efficiency of ICPs can be increased [7,30-32,41,72]. However, many ICPs still resort to 'shoe-leather epidemiology' because their hospitals lack the technologies for supporting the related HAI tasks [73]. Without the relevant HAI information needed for better communication and integration, the ICPs cannot enhance the effectiveness of HAI surveillance tasks. Accordingly, how to improve the work efficacy of ICPs by using the e-HAISIS will be in growing demand, as well as ways for better control and prevention of infectious diseases in healthcare settings.

Chapter III   Detection Model for HAI Surveillance and Control

3.1   Introduction

The HAI detection model is designed for detecting of the suspected HAI cases based on existing EMR systems of a hospital. For this study, we focused on healthcare-associated urinary tract infection (HAUTI), which is the most common type of HAI. Thus, taking good care of HAUTI is essential for the successful control of HAIs. In this chapter, we proposed an approach to build a detection model for surveillance of HAUTI based on the variables extracted from different EMR systems. First, we identified the surveillance variables that are available in the EMRs of the hospital based on the CDC's HAUTI case definitions and created rules for automatically extracting the variables from the EMRs. Then we performed discriminant analysis (DA) on a training set of EMRs with the extracted variables to construct a discriminant function (DF) for classifying patients into HAUTI and non-HAUTI groups. Finally, we evaluated the sensitivity, specificity and accuracy of the function using a testing set of EMRs.

3.2   Method

There were three steps involved in building a detection model for HAUTI surveillance and control. First of all, we mapped the CDC's HAUTI case definitions to a set of variables, and identified the variables whose values could be derived from the EMRs of the hospital automatically. Then with these variables we performed DA on a training set of the EMRs to construct a DF for the classification of a patient with or without HAUTI. Finally, we evaluated the sensitivity, specificity, and overall accuracy of the function using a testing set of EMRs.

3.3   Settings

This study was conducted at Taipei Medical University Wan Fang Hospital (TMUWFH), which is a 730-bed, tertiary-care teaching hospital in Taiwan. The hospital has an infection control team that consists of 6 certified ICPs: 1 infection control physician, 1 medical technologist, and 4 infection control nurses. The infection control practice follows CDC's 2009 published guidelines [13].

3.4 Data collection

All the patients who were admitted to the hospital from March 1st to June 30th, 2009 were included in the training set; all the patients who were admitted to the hospital from July 1st to October 31th, 2009 were included in the testing set. The patients in both sets were excluded if their length of stay was less than 48 hours. The HAUTI cases that were identified by the ICPs served as the gold standard for comparison. This study was approved by the IRB (Institution Review Board) of TMUWFH.

3.5 Extraction HAUTI variables from EMR systems

A joint team that consisted of ICPs and IT professionals was established in the hospital to map the CDC's HAUTI case definitions to the variables that were used for surveillance of HAUTI. First, we extracted as many variables as possible based on the CDC's HAUTI case definitions, including three HAUTI types: symptomatic urinary tract infection (SUTI), asymptomatic bacteriuria (ASB), and other urinary tract infections (OUTI). Then with these variables we created the mapping scheme for identifying ones whose value can be derived from EMRs automatically. An example of illustrating this mapping scheme, refer to Table 2. The left column describes one of the symptomatic urinary tract infection (SUTI) criteria; the right column shows the variables and the mapping rules that meet the criterion.

Table 2 : An example of mapping a CDC's HAUTI criterion to the variables and

associated rules

Symptomatic urinary tract infection criterion (1a)	Mapping rules
Patient had an indwelling urinary catheter (Invasive devices) in place at the time of specimen collection, and at least 1 of the following signs or symptoms with no other recognized cause:fever (>38℃), suprapubic tenderness, or costovertebral angle pain or tenderness, and a positive urine culture of $\geq 10^5$ colony-forming units (CFU)/ml with no more than 2 species of microorganisms.	x.SUTI = x.ID (Invasive device) AND (x.FEVER OR x.ST (suprapubic tenderness) OR x.CAP (costovertebral angle pain) OR x.Tenderness) AND x.PUC (positive urine culture) where x.Var represents a patient (x) with attribute (or variable) Var.

Each variable can have value '1 (True)' or '0 (False)', which can be derived in terms of medical procedures/medications/signs/symptoms recorded in the EMRs. For example, the value of variable 'ID (Invasive device)' for a patient x can be derived from the following rule:

if patient x had medical procedures for indwelling urinary catheter, cystoscopy, Percutaneous Nephrostomy (PCN), Double-J Catheter (DJ), or cystofix during his hospital stay

then x.ID = 1;

else x.ID = 0.

In other words, we can associate a variable with mapping rules that compute the value of the variable from the underlying EMRs. Since we wanted to reduce data collection efforts, the mapping rules must be executed automatically. For those mapping rules involving medical procedures/medications/signs/symptoms that were recorded with unstructured (i.e., free text formats) or not recorded in the EMRs, their corresponding variables would be excluded. Most signs and symptoms, except for fever, were recorded with unstructured or free text formats in the EMRs, and were not easily and correctly extracted. Similarly, physician reports and radiographic evidences of infection were not available as well [59]. Thus, we finally identified six variables, including fever, urine culture, blood culture, routine urinalysis, antibiotic use, and invasive devices, whose values could be derived from the EMRs of the hospital. The variables and associated data mapping rules are summarized in Table 3. The resulting rules associated with a criterion of the CDC's criteria for HAUTI case definitions would be more generic due to missing variables. Thus, we adopted discriminant analysis to approach a good solution based on the training set of EMRs.

Table 3 : The variables and associated data mapping rules

Variables (abbreviation)	Data mapping Rules
Fever (Fever)	IF a patient's temperature $>38^{\circ}\text{C}$ THEN Fever = '1' ELSE Fever = '0'
Urine culture (PUC)	IF(a patient has a positive urine culture test) THEN PUC = '1' ELSE PUC = '0'
Blood culture (PBC)	IF(a patient has a positive blood culture test) THEN PBC= '1' ELSE PBC = '0'
Routine urinalysis (PRU)	IF ((a patient has a positive urine dipstick for leukocyte esterase and/ or nitrate)* OR (a patient has positive WBC test)** OR (a patient has microorganisms seen on Gram stain of unspun urine)) THEN PRU = '1' ELSE PRU= '0'
Antibiotic use (AU)	IF (a patient is treated with oral or injection antibiotics but excluding the antibiotic use for prophylactic antibiotic premedication) THEN AU= '1' ELSE AU= '0'
Invasive device (ID)	IF (a patient has invasive devices such as Indwelling urinary catheter, cystoscopy, PCN, DJ, or cystofix) THEN ID= '1' ELSE ID= '0'

* Positive urine dipstick for leukocyte esterase or nitrate represents the test result with the value of '(+)'

** Positive WBC test represents the test result with the value of '1+', '2+', '3+', '4+', or 'NUMEROUS'

3.6 Building the HAUTI detection model

3.6.1 Discriminant analysis

We used the discriminant analysis (DA) for building the HAUTI detection model. The DA is a classification method that can construct a set of linear functions of independent variables, which are known as discriminant functions (DFs). These DFs can be used to predict group membership of a new observation. Although there are non-linear classification functions [74], the linear discriminant functions are simple, but powerful. Moreover, the non-linear classification functions require more computational resources, and they are costly to implement, in particular, for online operations. For a two-group classification problem, we need only one DF. Therefore, a patient can be classified into either the group with a HAUTI (UTI group) or without a HAUTI (non-UTI group). SPSS 15.0 statistical software was used to perform discriminant analysis.

3.6.2 Construction of the DF for predicting patients with HAUTI

The training data set consisted of 8,308 patients in which 133 were true HAUTI cases. In the DA, we firstly examine whether there are any significant differences between groups on each of the independent variables using group means and ANOVA results. In Table 4, the results of tests of equality of group means indicated that all variables significantly contribute (Sig. = .000) to the separation of UTI and non-UTI groups.

Table 4 : Tests of equality of group means

Variable	Wilks' Lambda	F	df1	df2	Sig.
Urine culture	0.911	1208.700	1	12313	.000
Blood culture	0.972	353.324	1	12313	.000
Fever	0.984	194.266	1	12313	.000
Antibiotic use	0.996	50.170	1	12313	.000
Invasive devices	0.976	297.431	1	12313	.000
Routine urinalysis	0.975	315.847	1	12313	.000

Since there were only two groups, namely UTI and non-UTI, we need only one DF. In the correlation analysis (Table 5), the eigenvalue of the function is 0.119, which will explain 100% of variance. Wilk's lambda indicates 89.3% of the total variance in the discriminant scores that were not explained by differences among groups. However, the Chi-square test shows there is a highly significant difference ($p<0.000$) between the groups' means (centroids), as shown in Table 6.

Table 5 : Eigenvalue of the function

Function	Eigenvalue	% of Variance	Cumulative %	Canonical Correlation
1	.119[a]	100.0	100.0	.326

[a.] First 1 canonical discriminant functions were used in the analysis.

Table 6 : Wilks's lambda

Test of function(s)	Wilks's lambda	Chi-square	df	Sig.
1	0.893	1386.657	6	.000

The standardized discriminant function coefficients is to assess the degree of impact of each variable on the DF. In Table 7, the coefficients associated with each respective variable were: fever (.246), antibiotic use (-.001), blood culture (.270), routine urinalysis (.100), invasive devices (.107), and urine culture (.754). The strongest predictor was urine culture. Blood culture and fever were the next in importance to the function.

Table 7 : Standardized Canonical Discriminant Function Coefficients

Variable	Function one
Fever	.246
antibiotic use	-.001
blood culture	.270
routine urinalysis	.100
Invasive devices	.107
urine culture	.754

SPSS creates an unstandardized canonical discriminant function with the coefficients to calculate discriminant score:

Discriminant score = -0.428 + 1.827 (fever) − 0.002 (antibiotic use) + 1.583 (blood culture) + 0.319 (routine urinalysis) + 0.772 (invasive devices) + 3.208 (urine culture)

The means of the discriminant score for non-UTI and UTI groups were -0.028 and 4.270, respectively. The cut-off point is the average distance (2.149) between the groups. Thus, if discriminant score was less than 2.149, then the patient will be assigned to non-UTI group. If discriminant score was more than or equal to 2.149, then the patient will be assigned to UTI group. The overall accuracy of the classification was 95.3% (Table 8). The cross validation produced the same results as the original classification.

Table 8 : Classification results of the training data set

Actual Group membership			Predicted Group Membership		Total
			UTI	Non-UTI	
Original[b]	Count	True UTI	132	1	133
		Non-UTI	389	7,786	8,175
	%	True UTI	99.25	0.75	100.0
		Non-UTI	4.76	95.24	100.0
Cross-validated[a,c]	Count	True UTI	132	1	133
		Non-UTI	389	7,786	8,175
	%	True UTI	99.25	0.75	100.0
		Non-UTI	4.76	95.24	100.0

a. Cross validation was performed only for those cases in the analysis. In the cross validation, each case was classified by the functions that were derived from all of the cases other than that case.
b. 95.3% of the original grouped cases were correctly classified.
c. 95.3% of the cross-validated grouped cases were correctly classified.

3.7 Evaluation of the HAUTI detection model

A testing set of the EMRs consisted of 11,251 patients. Among them, there were 93 patients with HAUTI, and 11,158 without. The patients with HAUTI were served as golden standards to compare with the DF, in order to compute sensitivity, specificity and overall accuracy. Sensitivity refers to the probability that a patient with HAUTI will test positive. Specificity refers to the probability that a patient without HAUTI will test negative. Overall accuracy is the probability that a patient will be correctly classified by a test; that is, the sum of the true positives plus true negatives divided by the total number of patients tested.

In testing set, The DF predicted 694 patients (Table 9) with a UTI (UTI group).

However, the actual or true positive (TP) UTI cases were 93, and the remainder (601) were false positive (FP). Similarly, the DF predicted 10,557 patients without a UTI (non-UTI group); of these, 10,557 were true negative (TN) and the false negative (FN) was 0 case. We defined sensitivity, specificity and overall accuracy as follows:

Sensitivity = TP ÷ (TP + FN);

Specificity = TN ÷ (TN + FP);

Overall accuracy = (TP + TN) ÷ (TP + FN + FP + TN)

Table 9 : Classification results of the testing data set

			Predicted Group Membership		
Actual Group membership			UTI	Non- UTI	Total
Original[a]	Count	True UTI	93 (TP)	0 (FN)	93
		Non-UTI	601 (FP)	10,557 (TN)	11,158
	%	True UTI	100	0	100.0
		Non-UTI	5.39	94.61	100.0
a. 94.65% of the original grouped cases were correctly classified.					

All measures of the detection model are shown in Table 9. Accordingly, the DF performed the classification with a high sensitivity to be 100%, specificity to be 94.61%, and the overall accuracy to be 94.65%. In other words, the DF that contained the six variables discriminated well between the two groups.

3.8 Summary

We utilized the EMR systems of a hospital to extract surveillance variables and built a discrimination function to detect suspected cases for HAUTI surveillance and control. The built model demonstrated high sensitivity, specificity and accuracy in the detection of HAUTIs while reducing the number of suspected cases that were detected. Moreover, based on this model, the data collection and suspected case detection can be performed automatically. Therefore, our approach can facilitate adoption of EMR systems for HAUTI surveillance and control; this is particularly applicable for the hospitals in which the EMR systems are built piece-by-piece.

Chapter IV   Development of an Integrated HAUTI Surveillance Information System

4.1   Introduction

As indicated in Chapter III, we have built a detection model for HAUTI surveillance and control. Furthermore, we developed an integrated hospital-associated urinary tract infection (HAUTI) surveillance information system (called iHAUTISIS) based on existing EMR systems for improving the work efficiency of ICPs. The iHAUTISIS automatically collects data relevant to HAUTI surveillance from the different EMR systems, detects the suspected HAUTI cases, and provides a visualization dashboard that helps ICPs make better surveillance plans and facilitate their surveillance work.

Currently, at TMUWFH the ICPs performed surveillance tasks based on the existing culture-based surveillance information system (eCBSIS). In order to measure the system performance, we created a generic model for comparing the ICPs' work efficiency when using the existing eCBSIS and iHAUTISIS, respectively. This model can demonstrate a patient's state (unsuspected, suspected, and confirmed) and corresponding time spent on surveillance tasks performed by ICPs for the patient in that state.

4.2   Method

In order to measure the different system performance, we created a generic work model, as described in Section 4.5, for comparing ICPs' work efficiency when using the eCBSIS and iHAUTISIS, respectively. Afterwards, we recruited four ICPs to perform surveillance tasks. Since the suspected cases can be detected using the two systems, ICPs start their surveillance tasks once the suspected patients were noticed. Thus, in this study, each ICP was asked to complete the surveillance tasks for 30 suspected HAUTI patients using the eCBSIS, and then complete another 30 suspected HAUTI patients using the iHAUTISIS. The former patients were called the eCBSIS group, and the latter were called the iHAUTISIS group. Therefore, there were 120 suspected HAUTI cases in the eCBSIS and iHAUTISIS group, respectively.

For each patient in the eCBSIS and iHAUTISIS group, for each state we recorded the time needed to complete the surveillance tasks associated with that state, respectively. Data analysis was performed using the two-way analysis of variance (ANOVA) test for comparison of time differences between the eCBSIS and iHAUTISIS group. Level of significance was accepted when $p < 0.05$. The statistics software SPSSTM 18.0 edition (SPSS, Chicago, IL, USA) was used for the analysis.

4.3 Settings

This study was conducted at Taipei Medical University Wan Fang Hospital (TMUWFH), which is a 730-bed, tertiary-care teaching hospital in Taiwan. The Infection Control Department (ICD) is responsible for HAI surveillance and control and has an existing eCBSIS to help ICPs perform HAI surveillance tasks. The ICD had 6 ICPs including 1 infection control physician, 1 medical technologist and 4 infection control nurses. The 4 infection control nurses have been certified by the Infection Control Society of Taiwan [75]. The infection control practice follows CDC's 2009 published guidelines [13].

4.4 Data collection

The patients were admitted to the hospital on and after November 1, 2010. To consistently compare the work efficiency between the eCBSIS and iHAUTISIS, we only used truly HAUTI cases. This study was approved by the Institutional Review Board at TMUWFH.

4.5 Generic work model for HAI surveillance

HAI surveillance involves active case-finding by infection control teams and clinicians, uses clinical case definitions and requires the collection of additional data to determine the infection source. The ICPs need to routinely collect the patients' clinical data and laboratory tests results, and then analyze the data based on the CDC's guidelines to determine whether the patients are HAI cases. In general, patients may have experienced three states from the time of hospital admission to the time of hospital discharge: unsuspected, suspected, and confirmed. Thus, we can use a state transition diagram to model the workflow of HAI surveillance (Figure 1) [76]. A circle represents a state, and the arrow line that connects two states indicates a transfer from the state without an arrow to the state with an arrow. Each state may be associated with a group of patients whose states are the same as that state, and a set of surveillance tasks that should be performed to the patients with that state. The performance of the HAI surveillance tasks on an individual patient may trigger the patient's state change. The trigger is labeled on the edge between a « from state » and a « to state ».

Patients admitted to a hospital are supposed to be non-HAI cases. They are assigned to « unsuspected » state. For a patient in « unsuspected » state, ICPs collect and analyze his/her data relevant to HAI. If the patient's conditions are likely to meet the HAI case definitions, and meet the 48 hour criterion, then he/she is suspected with HAUTI. The patient's state is changed from state « unsuspected » to « suspected ».

For each patient in « suspected » state, the ICPs usually check the collected data, review the patients' medical records in more detail, and further conduct bedside/onsite investigation to see whether the patient's conditions truly meet the CDC's HAUTI case definitions. If the patient is confirmed to be a true HAUTI case, then his/her state is changed from « suspected » to « confirmed » state. Similarly, if the patient is determined not to be a true HAUTI case, his/her state is changed to the state « unsuspected ». For each patient in « confirmed » state, the ICPs must complete his/her infection card for follow-ups or prevention procedures, and report the confirmed cases to the Taiwan CDC [77]. All the patients' conditions are continuously monitored. Moreover, if the patient still stays in the hospital because of other conditions, his/her state is changed to the state « unsuspected ». The surveillance workflow ends when the patient is discharged after treatment. The ICPs handle the changes to patients' states and coordinate surveillance tasks using pen and paper, or with the help of computer systems.

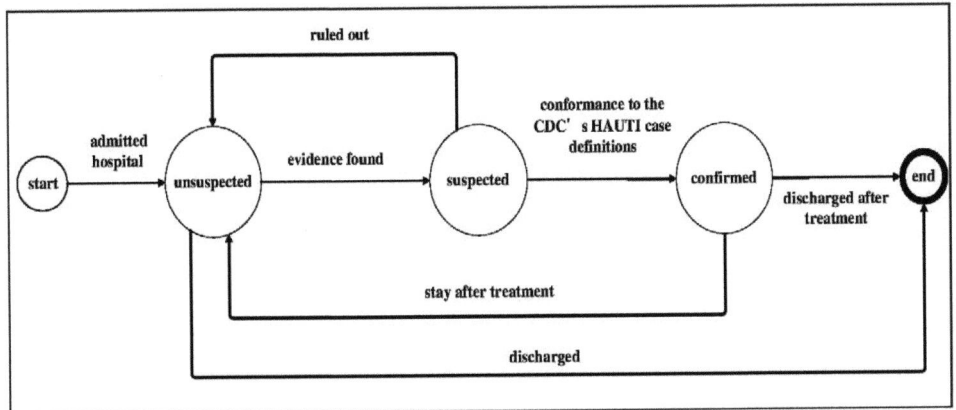

Figure 1 : A patient's state transition diagram

4.6 An Electronic culture-based HAUTI surveillance information system (eCBSIS)

The electronic culture-based surveillance information system (eCBSIS) used at TMUWFH includes several independent systems such as a laboratory information management system (LIS), inpatient management information system (IMIS), nursing information system (NIS), and other types of EMR systems, as shown in Figure 2. These systems partially support HAUTI surveillance information that can be accessed by ICPs just one at a time.

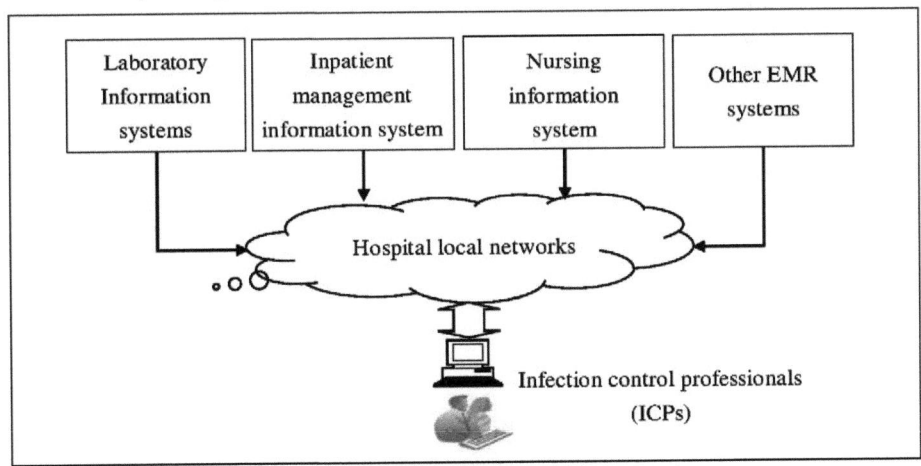

Figure 2 : The framework of the eCBSIS

ICPs use the LIS to collect patients' urine/blood culture tests and results. If the patients' culture results are positive, they are suspected to be HAUTI. The suspected patients are assigned to the ICPs for further investigation. In order to rule out the community-associated urinary tract infection (CAUTI), the ICPs can access the IMIS to acquire the patients' hospital admission records and the EMR systems to acquire their clinical data. The suspected patients are under comprehensive medical review and bedside investigation. If the patients' conditions meet the CDC's HAUTI case definitions, they are confirmed to be true HAUTI cases. The ICPs complete the true HAUTI patients' HAI cards for follow-up and prevention procedures. The required information can be acquired from the EMR systems. During hospitalization, all patients are routinely monitored by ICPs to ensure that HAI cases can be detected.

4.7 An Integrated HAUTI surveillance information system (iHAUTISIS)

The iHAUTISIS consists of case detection, data services, case management and visualization dashboard modules, as shown in Figure 3. It is designed for the integration of HAUTI surveillance data from existing EMR systems to support HAUTI surveillance practice.

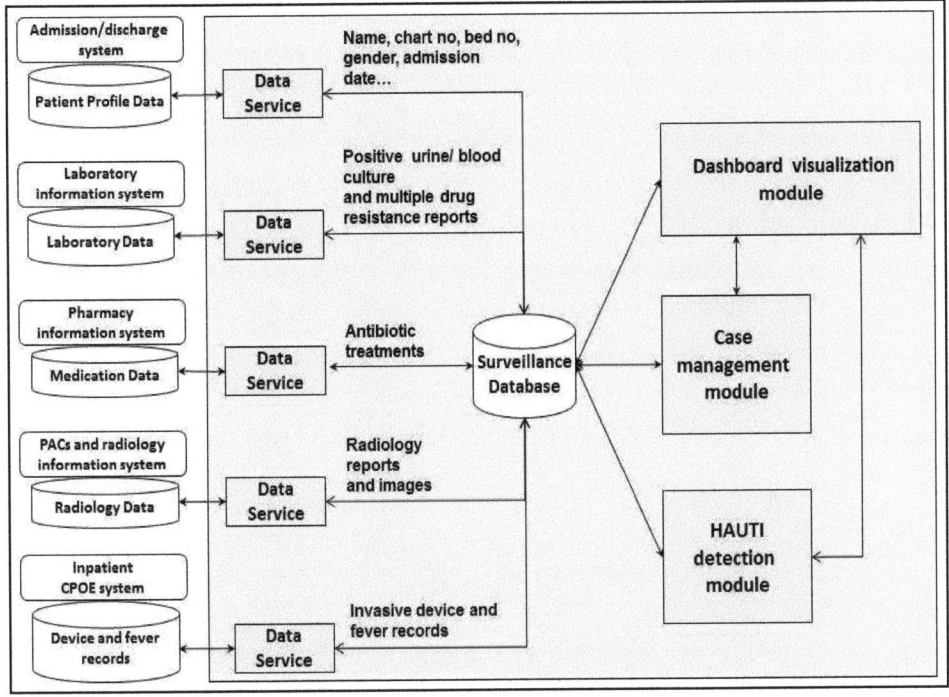

Figure 3 : The system architecture of the iHAUTISIS

The case detection module is primarily designed based on a discriminant function with six variables (fever, urine culture, blood culture, routine urinalysis, antibiotic use and invasive devices) for detection of suspected HAUTI cases [32]. A patient's discriminant score can be computed with the values of variables. If the patient's score is less than a cut-off point, then he/she is classified to a non-HAUTI case; otherwise he/she is classified to a HAUTI case.

The data services module, consisting of data collection service functions, is used to extract required surveillance data from EMR systems and transform them into standardized formats. Each data service is associated with a specific task for data retrieval and has standard interfaces to access the underlying EMR systems. There are six data collection service functions corresponding to the six surveillance variables (fever, urine culture, blood culture, routine urinalysis, antibiotic use, and invasive devices) as indicated in [32]. In addition, each patient's signs & symptoms and clinical data, such as patient profile, multiple drug resistance reports (MDRs), and radiology images and reports, are also collected. All data are integrated into the surveillance information database, as shown in Figure 3.

The case management module handles a patient's state change based on the patient state transition diagram (Figure 1). There are five major steps involved in the case management module as follows:

(i) When a patient is admitted, the case management module assigns « unsuspected » state to the patient, and initiates the HAUTI case detection module to monitor the patient's conditions.

(ii) When a patient is changed to « suspected » state, the case management module assigns « suspected » state to the patient, and sends an email and a short-message to the responsible ICP to conduct further chart review and bedside investigation.

(iii) When a patient is changed to « confirmed » state, the case management module assigns « confirmed » state to the patient, and sends a reminder to the responsible ICP to complete the patient's infection card by providing the patient's HAUTI related information such as clinical data, microbiology reports of culture results, and antibiogram, etc.

(iv) When a patient is excluded from a « suspected » case, the case management module assigns « unsuspected » state to the patient, and initiates the HAUTI case detection module to monitor the patient's conditions.

(v) After treatment, if a patient is discharged from the hospital, the case management module removes the patient from the state. However, if the patient still stays in the hospital because of other conditions, the case management module moves the patient to the « unsuspected » state.

To facilitate the ICPs with better management of patients and their states change during their hospitalization, we designed an integrated tabular view as a visualization dashboard (Figure 4). At the top of Figure 4, patients' clinical data are presented as variables displayed on « Application services » list. In this example, there are six variables: fever, urine culture (culture order (U)), blood culture (culture order (B)), routine urinalysis (Urine routine), antibiotic use (Anti) and invasive devices (UTI

28

devices). ICPs can select appropriate variables by dragging the variable tabs from the « Application services » list to the « Selected items » list. In this example, the selected items are fever and antibiotic use. The variables are then integrated with other patient information such as name, gender, bed number, etc., and displayed in the mid table area of the dashboard. If a variable is at a high/low risk of HAUTI, it is presented as a red icon (●)/green icon (●). For example, if a patient's temperature is more than 38 °C, then the variable, fever, is presented as a red icon (●), as shown in Figure 4.

At the very top of Figure 4, the patients are grouped into « unsuspected », « suspected » and « confirmed ». For example, if « suspected » tab is clicked, all the patients in « suspected » state are listed in the table. An ICP can browse an individual patient's detailed clinical data by clicking the tab (⬛). A window is then popped up, as shown in Figure 5, to show more detailed surveillance information, including patient profile, antibiotic treatments, fever records, white blood cell count (WBC) results, invasive device use records, culture and MDR reports, and chest images/reports. If the tab « culture reports and MDR » is clicked, the popup window presents the patient's culture tests history. If we want to know the detailed MDR report of a test, we can click the « detail » tab (under MDR column) associated with that test.

Although the system can automatically detect a suspected HAUTI case, the ICPs still need to make a decision on whether the suspected case is a true case. Thus, if ICPs confirm a suspected HAUTI case to be a true case, the ICP can click the ⬛ icon to move the patient to the « confirmed » group, or otherwise click the ⬛ icon to move the patient to the « unsuspected » group.

We adopted Adobe Flex technology to implement the visualization of surveillance information, which can run on all major browsers using Adobe Flash Player software [78]. Therefore, ICPs can use a laptop or mobile devices to access the system and the patients' HAUTI related information to perform HAUTI surveillance tasks at any time and anywhere, as shown in Figure 5.

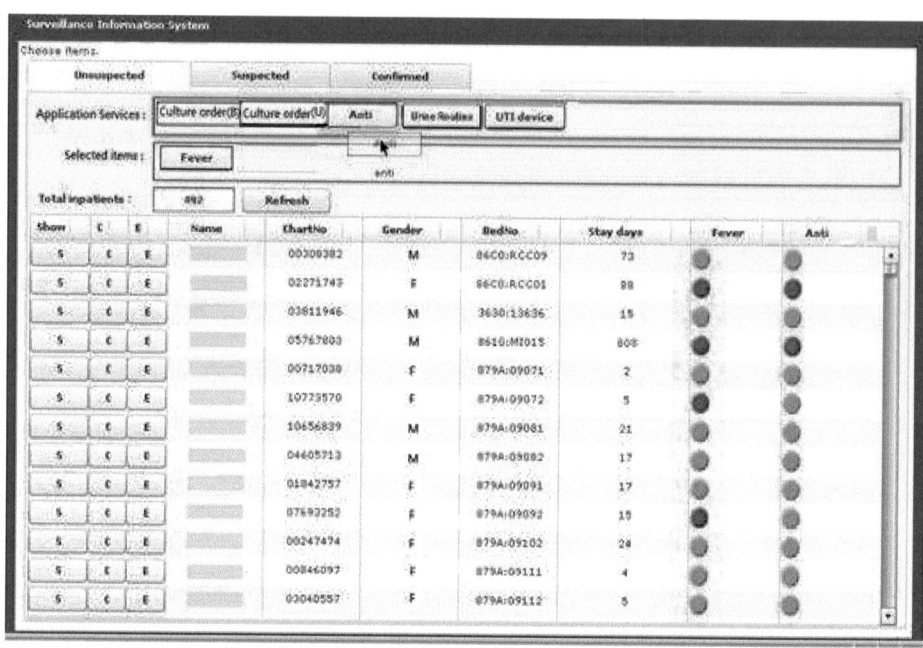

Figure 4 : The visualization dashboard with an integrated tabular view

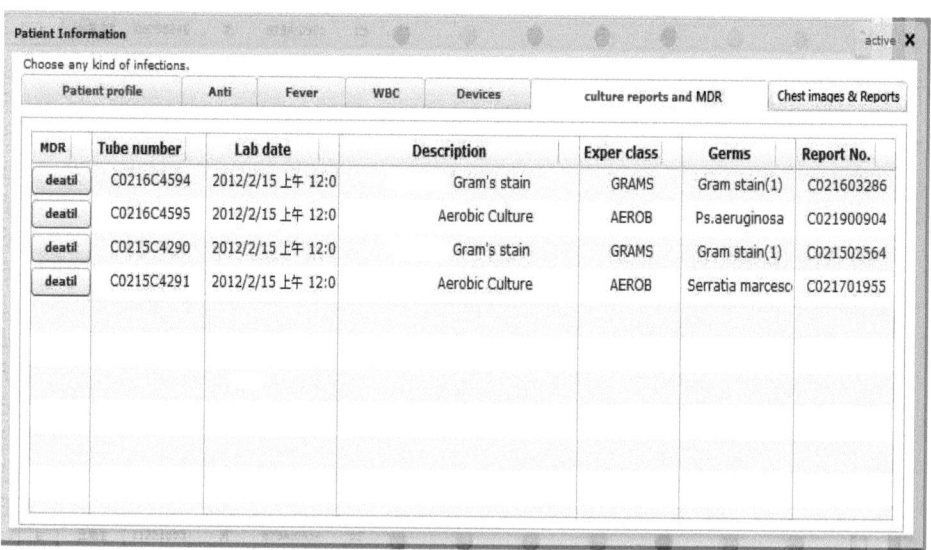

Figure 5 : The surveillance data relevant to HAUTI of an individual patient

30

4.8 Comparison of work efficiency

With the support of different systems, ICPs may perform varied tasks for their HAI surveillance practice. Thus, we used the generic HAI model presented in Section 4.5 as a common ground to compare the surveillance tasks required to perform when using the two different systems. When using the eCBSIS and iHAUTISIS to support HAUTI surveillance, we can compare the surveillance tasks performed by ICPs for each patient state. Table 10 summarizes three surveillance task groups corresponding to the three patient states when using the eCBSIS and iHAUTISIS, respectively. For example, to detect a suspected patient from the unsuspected group, an ICP has to check the patient's culture tests results when using the eCBSIS; however, the ICP does not need to do anything when using the iHAUTISIS because the system can detect the suspected cases automatically.

Table 10 : The patient states and corresponding surveillance tasks

Patient state	Surveillance tasks	Surveillance systems	
		eCBSIS	iHAUTISIS
Unsuspected	1. Collect the patients' surveillance data; 2. Detect suspected HAUTI cases.	1. ICPs use a LIS to screen the patients with positive culture tests results, and use the IMIS for the patients' admission information. 2. If the patients with positive culture tests results and meet the 48 hour criterion, they are suspected HAUTI patients.	1. Suspected patients are detected by the system automatically. 2. ICPs view the patients' admission information by clicking on the dashboard, and rule out the patients who don't meet the 48 hour criterion.

		1. ICPs access different EMR systems for the surveillance information one at a time to support chart review and bedside investigation. 2. For those information that cannot be acquired from EMR systems, the ICPs perform chart review & bedside investigation manually. 3. Justify the evidences and confirm the true HAUTI cases.	1. ICPs access the integrated surveillance data through the visualization dashboard to support chart review & bedside investigation. 2. For those information that cannot be acquired from the EMR systems, the ICPs perform chart review & bedside investigation manually. 3. Justify the evidences and confirm the true HAUTI cases.
Suspected	1.Perform comprehensive chart review and bedside investigation; 2. Confirm the true HAUTI cases.		
Confirmed	Complete the true HAUTI patients' HAI cards, and report the patients to Taiwan CDC.	1. ICPs complete the true HAUTI patients' HAI cards manually. 2. The confirmed HAUTI cases reporting is also done manually.	The iHAUTISIS can generate a true HAUTI cases list to help ICPs complete the true HAUTI patients' HAI cards and reporting.

4.9 Evaluation results

This study started on November 1, 2010 and ended on April 22, 2011. Each of ICPs should collect 30 suspected HAUTI patients by using eCBSIS and iHAUTISIS, respectively. Therefore, there were 120 suspected HAUTI cases in the eCBSIS and iHAUTISIS group, respectively. To compare the eCBSIS with iHAUTISIS, we only used truly HAUTI cases. Accordingly, of these, there were 35 and 69 true HAUTI

33

cases identified in the eCBSIS and iHAUTISIS group, respectively. The time spent on each patient state of the two groups is presented descriptively in Table 11. The time spent on unsuspected, suspected and confirmed states in the iHAUTISIS and eCBSIS groups were 73.31±20.71 and 165.95±78.24, 134.83±73.76 and 175.44±85.56, and 134.63±39.61 and 221.22±85.42 seconds, respectively. The marginal means in the iHAUTISIS and eCBSIS groups were 114.26±57.43 and 187.54±84.87 seconds, respectively. We can see the time cost in the eCBSIS group was much greater than that in the iHAUTISIS group.

Table 11 : Descriptive statistics

System	iHAUTISIS (N=69)		eCBSIS (N=35)	
Patient state	Mean (sec.)	SD	Mean (sec.)	SD
Unsuspected	73.31	20.71	165.95	78.24
Suspected	134.83	73.76	175.44	82.58
Confirmed	134.63	39.61	221.22	85.42
Marginal mean(Total)	114.26	57.43	187.54	84.87

N = number of true HAUTI cases to be identified by the eCBSIS and iHAUTI systems, respectively.

sec., seconds; SD, Standard Deviation.

The test of homogeneity of variance between the eCBSIS and iHAUTISIS groups was statistically significant (p>0.05). That is, the assumption of the ANOVA test has been met. We then performed the two-way ANOVA (Table 12). We can see the interaction between system group and patient state (F=4.818, p=0.009) was statistically significant. That means, on one hand some changes in both independent variables (surveillance system * patient state) must have an effect on the dependent variable (time cost); on the other hand it cannot explain which surveillance system behaved differently. This is because the existing hospital's EMR systems do not support all of the HAUTI surveillance data, such as most clinical signs and symptoms. Therefore, for each patient's state, the ICPs' degree of use of the surveillance system is different. For example, although the patient's surveillance data can be partially acquired from the surveillance systems in the « suspected » state,

34

ICPs sometimes may spend more time on performing manual chart review and bedside investigation. On the contrary, with the patients in the « suspected » state, the ICPs can use the surveillance systems to capture the suspected HAUTI cases rather than manually.

Table 12 : Tests of between-subjects effects

Dependent variable: time cost					
Source	Type III sum of squares	df	Mean square	F	Sig.
Corrected model	608729.70[a]	5	121745.94	31.21	0.00
Intercept	6344895.96	1	6344895.96	1626.30	0.00
Surveillance system	374073.73	1	374073.73	95.88	0.00
Patient state	160323.22	2	80161.61	20.55	0.00
Surveillance system * patient state	37596.00	2	18798.00	4.82	0.01
Error	1193839.05	306	3901.44		
Total	7823653.28	312			
Corrected total	1802568.75	311			
a. $R^2 = 0.338$ (adjusted $R^2 = 0.327$)					
Sig., significance.					

Therefore, we used post-hoc comparisons to test the marginal mean of each patient state between system groups. The results are shown in Table 13. There were three pairwise comparisons, which had statistically significant difference between systems ($p < 0.05$), respectively. We can see that the time spent on all three patient states in the iHAUTISIS group was statistically significant and less than in the eCBSIS group.

Table 13 : Pairwise comparisons

Dependent variable: time cost							
Patient state	(I) surveillance system	(J) surveillance system	Mean difference (I - J) *	Std error	Sig[a]	95% CI for the difference[a]	
						Lower bound	Upper bound
Unsuspected	iHAUTISIS	eCBSIS	-92.64	10.01	0.000	-112.49	-72.78
	eCBSIS	iHAUTISIS	92.64	10.01	0.000	72.78	112.49
Suspected	iHAUTISIS	eCBSIS	-40.61	15.94	0.012	-72.23	-9.00
	eCBSIS	iHAUTISIS	40.61	15.94	0.012	9.00	72.23
Confirmed	iHAUTISIS	eCBSIS	-86.59	12.24	0.000	-110.86	-62.31
	eCBSIS	iHAUTISIS	86.59	12.24	0.000	62.31	110.86
Based on estimated marginal means.							
* The mean difference was significant at the 0.05 level							
[a] Adjusted multiple comparisons: Bonferroni.							
CI, confidence interval; Sig, significance; Std, Standard.							

4.10 Summary

In this study, we developed an iHAUTISIS with a visualization dashboard for facilitating the HAUTI surveillance tasks and reducing ICPs' workload. The system can collect data relevant to HAUTI surveillance from the different EMR systems automatically. We also proposed a generic model as a common ground for comparisons between different systems, in terms of a patient's state and the time spent on the surveillance tasks performed by ICPs for the patient in that state. This makes comparisons more precise and understandable.

With increased adoption of EMR systems, the development of the integrated HAI surveillance information systems would be more and more cost-effective. Moreover, the iHAUTISIS adopted web-based technology that enables ICPs using laptops or mobile devices to online access a patient's surveillance information. Thus, the system can further facilitate the HAI surveillance.

Chapter V   Discussions

In recent years, an increasing number of ICPs have adopted EMR systems to support routinely HAI surveillance and control. Some ICPs have utilized laboratory information systems to identify the patients with positive culture tests so that a further bedside investigation can be performed [40,54,55,64,67]. Some of the ICPs associated the laboratory or microbiology data with the diagnostic, demographic, and clinical guidelines to generate alerts for the critical laboratory values and recommendations for the best antibiotic practices [8,79]. Some other ICPs have linked the patients who produce positive culture tests to their clinical and admission data to facilitate the chart review and bedside investigation [31,41,65,71], while other ICPs have monitored the patients' conditions by using their clinical data, such as their culture tests, prescribed antibiotics (antibiotic treatment), and associated invasive devices, or a combination of these clinical data to identify the patients who are involved in suspected HAI cases [29,30,80]. However, it still remains a significant challenge to build a flexible and effective detection model, which can keep pace with ever growing EMR systems adopted by a hospital.

In Chapter III presented here, we demonstrated a series of steps to construct a detection model for the prediction of suspected HAUTI cases based on existing EMRs of a hospital. We first identified as many variables as possible that were available in the hospital EMR systems for HAI surveillance. Then we created rules to map the variables defined by the CDC's guidelines into the ones presented in the EMRs, and finally with the variables we tested their discrimination power, and constructed the detection model using discriminate analysis. Unlike the previous studies that only used a single or a logical combination of surveillance variables to achieve different levels of sensitivity for capturing HAI cases, our approach identified the importance of the variable and made use of these variables to build DFs. Thus, the function described the classification more precisely. Consequently, the number of the predicted suspected UTI cases was relatively small; this can reduce the time and effort required to perform bedside investigations and chart reviews.

Based on the discriminant analysis, the cut-off point of the UTI and non-UTI groups was 2.149. That means, a patient with discriminant score, which was more than or equal to 2.149, would be assigned to the UTI group, and the patient with the score, which was less than 2.149 would be assigned to the non-UTI group. The coefficient of a variable with larger value in the discriminant function, it would have stronger impact on the discriminant score if the variable is true. In this study we can see that the impacts of the variables from strongest to the weakest are urine culture, blood culture, fever, routine urinalysis, invasive device, and antibiotic use. This might actually reflect medical treatments for hospitalized patients in Taiwan. The more common treatments may lead to the weaker discrimination power. The coefficient with negative (positive) value tends to result in lower (larger) discriminant score. This may increase the chances of the patient to be assigned to the non-UTI (UTI) group.

The HAI surveillance method currently used by TMUWFH is primarily based on the positive culture tests. To compare our approach with the currently used surveillance method, we looked more closely at the testing set, which consisted of 2,303 patients who displayed positive urine culture tests. Therefore, with the currently used method, we had to investigate 2,303 (20.46%) patients, and we identified 93 true UTI cases. However, by using the approach presented here, we only had to investigate 694 (6.16%) patients, and we also identified 93 true UTI cases. In this example, our approach effectively reduced 69.86 % of the investigation effort when compared to the current method. The comparison of the above mentioned two methods are summarized in Table 14.

Table 14 : Summary of the comparisons

Surveillance methods[a]	# of cases to be investigated	UTI cases detected	Sensitivity	Specificity
Currently used surveillance method	2,303 (20.46%)	93	100.00%	80%
The present HAUTI approach	694 (6.16%)	93	100.00%	94.61%
a. There were 11,251 total cases and 93 total true HAUTI cases				

Moreover, the positive predictive value (PPV) of the current used surveillance method and the present HAUTI detection model was 4% and 13%, respectively (Table 15). In our detection approach, the PPV increased from 4% to 13%; however, it showed that the detection algorithm is not good enough for true HAUTI recognition.

Table 15 : Positive predictive value of the currently used surveillance method and the

present

Surveillance methods[a]	# of cases to be investigated	Truly HAUTI cases detected	False HAUTI cases detected	PPV[b]
Currently used surveillance method	2,303 (20.46%)	93	2,210	4%
The present HAUTI approach	694 (6.16%)	93	601	13%
a. There were 11,251 total cases and 93 total true HAUTI cases				
b. PPV, positive predictive value				

Surveillance for Catheter-associated urinary tract infection (CAUTI) is performed in at least one inpatient location in the healthcare institution for at least one calendar month as indicated in the Patient Safety Monthly Reporting Plan (CDC 57.106) [13]. Although CDC guidelines recommend that surveillance for HAUTI should be performed at least once a month, our approach allows more frequent surveillance for HAUTI.

Since hospitals may adopt their EMR systems with different functionalities to meet their requirements, the surveillance variables that can be extracted from the EMR systems may differ. Our approach uses the surveillance variables that are available in the EMR systems of each hospital, and automatically extracts the variable values using the mapping rules. Referring to our approach, the hospitals can rebuild the discriminant functions using their training sets. When more EMR systems have been adopted, more surveillance variables can be included in this model. Therefore, our approach can facilitate the adoption of EMR systems for HAUTI surveillance and control; this is particularly applicable for the hospitals in which the EMR systems are built piece-by-piece.

As previous studies indicated, the eCBSIS can reduce 60% to 65% of time spent on the surveillance work with respect to the conventional (manual) surveillance methods [41,65]. Furthermore, in Chapter IV, we have developed an iHAUTISIS for mitigating ICPs' surveillance workload. This system can collect data relevant to HAUTI surveillance from different EMR systems automatically. We also designed an integrated tabular view as the visualization dashboard that enabled ICPs to get an at-a-glance overview and details of their surveillance work. For example, a patient with more red icons has higher risk of HAUTI. Then, ICPs can prioritize screening those suspected HAUTI cases based on red icons. Therefore, the visualization dashboard can help ICPs make better surveillance plans and facilitate their surveillance work. However, in this study the ICPs were still required to perform chart review and bedside investigation manually when using the eCBSIS and iHAUTISIS, respectively. This is because the existing EMR systems do not support all of the HAUTI surveillance data. For example, most signs and symptoms were not recorded in the EMR systems. Nevertheless, according to the study results (Table 13), it showed that the iHAUTISIS performed better than the eCBSIS in terms of ICPs' time cost. The iHAUTISIS can reduce 73.27 seconds (114.26 vs. 187.53 seconds); in other words, it can effectively reduce 39% time cost for each patient on average. In practice, the time spent on HAI surveillance includes not only the time spent on system operations but also the time spent on the relevant data collection and preparation, and communications between healthcare professionals, which consume most of the ICPs' time. Thus, ICPs can save even more time by using the iHAUTISIS. The saved time can be used for patient care and promotion of HAI prevention.

Unlike previous studies, this study used a generic HAI model for measuring the work efficiency of different electronic surveillance systems. The model provides a common ground for comparisons, in terms of a patient's state and the time spent on surveillance tasks performed by ICPs for the patient in that state, between different systems. This made the comparisons more precise and understandable.

More importantly, unlike the eCBSIS that prints out the patients' culture tests results and provides suspected cases passively, the iHAUTISIS can automatically detect a suspected HAUTI patient, and send an alert through email or a short message service to the responsible ICPs. Therefore, ICPs can respond faster and conduct HAI surveillance tasks earlier.

With increased adoption of EMR systems, more and more HAI surveillance data are available. In other words, the integrated HAI surveillance information systems would be more and more cost-effective because data collection and case finding can be done automatically. Moreover, the iHAUTISIS adopted web-based technology that enables ICPs to online access a patient's surveillance information using laptops or mobile devices. This can enhance ICPs' surveillance capability and free-up time to conduct proactive HAI preventive activities.

Chapter VI Conclusions and Future Work

6.1 Conclusions

Adoption of EMR systems for supporting clinical services is essential in improving healthcare quality and patient safety. More and more healthcare providers (hospitals) have been encouraged to adopt EMR systems gradually over time. In this study, we have demostrated a series of steps to construct a detection model for the prediction of suspected HAUTI cases based on existing EMRs of a hospital. In our approach presented here, the built detection model is more flexible and can make use of as many variables available in EMR systems as possible. In other words, the built detection model can keep pace with ever growing EMR systems adopted by hospitals.

More importantly, our approach can differentiate the importance of the adopted variables in the DF for prediction of the suspected HAUTI cases. Moreover, the built model demonstrated high sensitivity and specificity in the detection of HAUTI cases while reducing the number of suspected cases detected. With the approach, data collection and suspected case finding can be done automatically. Accordingly, this allows ICPs to reduce time and effort spent on HAI surveillance, and to increase time and effort spent on HAI control and prevention.

With increased adoption of EMR systems, the development of the e-HAISISs might become more and more cost-effective. Therefore, we look forward to further development of an iHAUTISIS for mitigating ICPs' surveillance workload. The iHAUTISIS with a visualization dashboard can facilitate the HAUTI surveillance tasks and reduce the ICPs' workload. The main idea was that the ICPs can get an at-a-glance overview of what's happening with these suspected HAUTI cases. Thus, the ICPs can immediately see each suspected HAUTI case with red/green icons and know if his/her corresponding conditions have met the CDC's HAUTI case definitions or not. Then ICPs can prioritize screening those suspected HAUTI cases that have more red icons.

Furthermore, we also proposed a generic model as a common ground for comparisons between different systems, in terms of a patient's state and the time

42

spent on the surveillance tasks performed by ICPs for the patient in that state. This makes comparisons more precise and understandable.

The iHAUTISIS can collect data relevant to HAUTI surveillance from the different EMR systems and detects the suspected HAUTI cases automatically. Also, it can support ICPs to achieve better case management and to replace paperwork. Therefore, the daily HAI surveillance tasks can be performed more effectively and automatically. In the future, the ICPs might have more opportunities to transform routine surveillance tasks into proactive preventive activities.

6.2 Future work

The detection accuracy and work efficacy are described in this study, respectively. Referring to the accuracy of the detection model, it can reach high sensitivity and specificity while reducing the number of suspected cases detected (from 2,303 to 694). However, if more and more EMRs can be improved, more electronic surveillance variables might be used for our detection model, such as patients' signs and symptoms. Accordingly, the detection algorithms may be modified to make the PPV more precise. Moreover, the different detection models should be developed for other types of HAI, such as BSI, RTI, and SSI. Thus, extending the completeness of detection to all HAIs will improve patient safety and healthcare quality.

Furthermore, the implementation of iHAUTISIS can be done for BSI, RTI, and SSI, as well. Therefore, the effectiveness of ICPs' performance can be continually improved. With increased adoption of EMR systems, the relevant HAI data becomes diversified and enormous, and can be easily delivered to ICPs in the near future. For example, it can be delivered by a bedside monitor continuously measuring vital signs parameters, or by a respirator measuring the saturated percentage of oxygen in the blood. Therefore, it might be interesting to design a good interface for ICPs and to further study how to retrieve heterogeneous/enormous data sources, how to integrate the different data types, and how to transform HAI data into useful information.

Reference

1. McKibben, L., Horan, T., Tokars, J. I., Fowler, G., Cardo, D. M., Pearson, M. L., ... & Healthcare Infection Control Practices Advisory Committee. (2005). Guidance on public reporting of healthcare-associated infections: recommendations of the Healthcare Infection Control Practices Advisory Committee. *American Journal of Infection Control, 33*(4), 217-226.

2. World Health Organization. (2011). Report on the burden of endemic health care-associated infection worldwide. *Geneva: World Health Organization*, 1-34.

3. Siempos, I. I., Fragoulis, K. N., & Falagas, M. E. (2007). World Wide Web resources on control of nosocomial infections. *Journal of Crit Care, 11*(1), 101.

4. World Health Organization (Ed.). (2009). Global health risks: mortality and burden of disease attributable to selected major risks. *Geneva, Switzerland: World Health Organization.*

5. Roy, M. C., & Perl, T. M. (1997). Basics of surgical-site infection surveillance. *Infection Control and Hospital Epidemiology*, 659-668.

6. Gaynes RP , Horan TC. Surveillance of nosocomial infections. In: Mayhall CG, editor. Hospital Epidemiology and Infection Control. Philadelphia, PA:Williams & Wilkins; 1997.

7. Wright, M. O., Fisher, A., John, M., Reynolds, K., Peterson, L. R., & Robicsek, A. (2009). The electronic medical record as a tool for infection surveillance: successful automation of device-days. *American Journal of Infection Control,37*(5), 364-370.

8. Atreja, A., Gordon, S. M., Pollock, D. A., Olmsted, R. N., & Brennan, P. J. (2008). Opportunities and challenges in utilizing electronic health records for infection surveillance, prevention, and control. *American Journal of Infection Control, 36*(3), S37-S46.

9. Hillestad, R., Bigelow, J., Bower, A., Girosi, F., Meili, R., Scoville, R., & Taylor, R. (2005). Can electronic medical record systems transform health care? Potential health benefits, savings, and costs. *Health Affairs, 24*(5), 1103-1117.

10. Shiffman, R. N., Brandt, C. A., Liaw, Y., & Corb, G. J. (1999). A design model for computer-based guideline implementation based on information management

services. *Journal of the American Medical Informatics Association, 6*(2), 99-103.

11. Garner, J. S., Jarvis, W. R., Emori, T. G., Horan, T. C., & Hughes, J. M. (1988). CDC definitions for nosocomial infections, 1988. *American Journal of Infection Control, 16*(3), 128-140.

12. Horan TC, Gaynes RP. Surveillance of nosocomial infections. In: Mayhall CG, editor. Hospital epidemiology and infection control. 3rd ed. Philadelphia: Lippincott Williams & Wilkins; 2004. pp. 1659–702.

13. Centers for Disease Control. (2013). CDC/NHSN surveillance definition of healthcare-associated infection and criteria for specific types of infections in the acute care setting. *National Healthcare Safety Network, Washington.*

14. HALEY, R. W., CULVER, D. H., WHITE, J. W., Morgan, W. M., Emori, T. G., Munn, V. P., & HOOTON, T. M. (1985). The efficacy of infection surveillance and control programs in preventing nosocomial infections in US hospitals. *American Journal of Epidemiology, 121*(2), 182-205.

15. Widmer, A. F. (1994). Infection control and prevention strategies in the ICU. *Intensive Care Medicine, 20*(4), S7-S11.

16. Klevens, R. M., Edwards, J. R., Richards, C. L., Horan, T. C., Gaynes, R. P., Pollock, D. A., & Cardo, D. M. (2007). Estimating health care-associated infections and deaths in US hospitals, 2002. *Public Health Reports, 122*(2), 160.

17. US Department of Health and Human Services (2013). *National action plan to prevent healthcare-associated infections: Roadmap to elimination.* Retrieved from http://www.health.gov/hai/prevent_hai.asp#hai (accessed 7 Mar 2014).

18. World Health Organization. *Health care-associated infections FACT SHEET.* Retrieved from http://www.who.int/gpsc/country_work/gpsc_ccisc_fact_sheet_en.pdf (accessed 3 Sep 2014).

19. Centers for Disease Control of Taiwan. *Statistics & Analysis.* Retrieved from http://www.cdc.gov.tw/public/Attachment/7121715371571.pdf (accessed 7 Aug 2009).

20. Burke, J. P. (2003). Infection control-a problem for patient safety. *New England Journal of Medicine, 348*(7), 651-656.

21. Turner, J. (1992). Hand-washing behavior versus hand-washing guidelines in the ICU. *Heart & Lung: The Journal of Critical Care*, *22*(3), 275-277.

22. Montecalvo, M. A., Jarvis, W. R., Uman, J., Shay, D. K., Petrullo, C., Horowitz, H. W., & Wormser, G. P. (2001). Costs and savings associated with infection control measures that reduced transmission of vancomycin-resistant enterococci in an endemic setting. *Infection Control and Hospital Epidemiology*, *22*(7), 437-442.

23. Harbarth, S., Sax, H., & Gastmeier, P. (2003). The preventable proportion of nosocomial infections: an overview of published reports. *Journal of Hospital infection*, *54*(4), 258-266.

24. Sax, H., Hugonnet, S., Harbarth, S., Herrault, P., & Pittet, D. (2001). Variation in nosocomial infection prevalence according to patient care setting: a hospital-wide survey. *Journal of Hospital infection*, *48*(1), 27-32.

25. Centers for Disease Control (US). *National Healthcare Safety Network (NHSN)*. Retrieved from http://www.cdc.gov/nhsn/pdfs/outlineforHAIsurveillance.pdf (Access 5 May 2013).

26. Lo, Y. S., Lee, W. S., Chen, G. B., & Liu, C. T. (2014). Improving the work efficiency of healthcare-associated infection surveillance using electronic medical records. *Computer Methods and Programs in Biomedicine*, *117*(2), 351-359.

27. Glenister, H. M., Taylor, L. J., Bartlett, C. L. R., Cooke, E. M., Sedgwick, J. A., & Mackintosh, C. A. (1993). An evaluation of surveillance methods for detecting infections in hospital inpatients. *Journal of Hospital Infection*, *23*(3), 229-242.

28. WENZEL, R. P., OSTERMAN, C. A., HUNTING, K. J., & GWALTNEY, J. M. (1976). Hospital-Acquired infections I. Surveillance in A university hospital. *American Journal of Epidemiology*, *103*(3), 251-260.

29. McNamara, M. J., Hill, M. C., BALOWS, A., & TUCKER, E. B. (1967). A study of the bacteriologic patterns of hospital infections. *Annals of Internal Medicine*,*66*(3), 480-488.

30. Willard, K. E., Johnson, J. R., & Connelly, D. P. (1996). Radical improvements in the display of clinical microbiology results: a Web-based clinical information

system. *The American Journal of Medicine, 101*(5), 541-549.

31. Bouam, S., Girou, E., Brun-Buisson, C., Karadimas, H., & Lepage, E. (2003). An intranet-based automated system for the surveillance of nosocomial infections: prospective validation compared with physicians' self-reports. *Infection Control and Hospital Epidemiology, 24*(1), 51-55.

32. Lo, Y. S., Lee, W. S., Chen, G. B., & Liu, C. T. (2014). Improving the work efficiency of healthcare-associated infection surveillance using electronic medical records. *Computer Methods and Programs in Biomedicine, 117*(2), 351-359.

33. Centers for Disease Control. *MMWR: Overview of Syndromic Surveillance: What is Syndromic Surveillance?.* Retrieved from http://www.cdc.gov/mmwr/preview/mmwrhtml/su5301a3.htm (accessed 7 May 2013).

34. de Bruin, J. S., Seeling, W., & Schuh, C. (2014). Data use and effectiveness in electronic surveillance of healthcare associated infections in the 21st century: a systematic review. *Journal of the American Medical Informatics Association,* doi:10.1136/amiajnl-2013-002089.

35. Cadwallader, H. L., Toohey, M., Linton, S., Dyson, A., & Riley, T. V. (2001). A comparison of two methods for identifying surgical site infections following orthopaedic surgery. *Journal of Hospital Infection, 48*(4), 261-266.

36. Yokoe, D. S., Christiansen, C. L., Johnson, R., Sands, K. E., Livingston, J., Shtatland, E. S., & Platt, R. (2001). Epidemiology of and surveillance for postpartum infections. *Emerging Infectious Diseases, 7*(5), 837.

37. Moro, M. L., & Morsillo, F. (2004). Can hospital discharge diagnoses be used for surveillance of surgical-site infections?. *Journal of Hospital Infection, 56*(3), 239-241.

38. Yokoe, D. S., Noskin, G. A., Cunningham, S. M., Zuccotti, G., Plaskett, T., Fraser, V. J., ... & Platt, R. (2004). Enhanced identification of postoperative infections among inpatients. *Emerging Infectious Diseases, 10*(11), 1924.

39. Spolaore, P., Pellizzer, G., Fedeli, U., Schievano, E., Mantoan, P., Timillero, L., & Saia, M. (2005). Linkage of microbiology reports and hospital discharge

diagnoses for surveillance of surgical site infections. *Journal of Hospital Infection*, 60(4), 317-320.

40. Brossette, S. E., Hacek, D. M., Gavin, P. J., Kamdar, M. A., Gadbois, K. D., Fisher, A. G., & Peterson, L. R. (2006). A Laboratory-Based, Hospital-Wide, Electronic Marker for Nosocomial Infection The Future of Infection Control Surveillance?. *American Journal of Clinical Pathology*, 125(1), 34-39.

41. Chalfine, A., Gonot, J., Nadine Calvo-Verjat, M. D., Dazza, F. E., Billuart, O., Kitzis, M. D., ... & Carlet, J. (2006). Highly sensitive and efficient computer-assisted system for routine surveillance for surgical site infection. *Infection Control and Hospital Epidemiology*, 27(8), 794-801.

42. Leth, R. A., & Møller, J. K. (2006). Surveillance of hospital-acquired infections based on electronic hospital registries. *Journal of Hospital Infection*, 62(1), 71-79.

43. Sherman, E. R., Heydon, K. H., John, K. H. S., Eva Teszner, B. S. N., Rettig, S. L., Alexander, S. K., ... & Coffin, S. E. (2006). Administrative data fail to accurately identify cases of healthcare-associated infection. *Infection Control and Hospital Epidemiology*, 27(4), 332-337.

44. Bolon, M. K., Hooper, D., Stevenson, K. B., Greenbaum, M., Olsen, M. A., Herwaldt, L., ... & Yokoe, D. S. (2009). Improved surveillance for surgical site infections after orthopedic implantation procedures: extending applications for automated data. *Clinical Infectious Diseases*, 48(9), 1223-1229.

45. Leth, R. A., Nørgaard, M., Uldbjerg, N., Thomsen, R. W., & Møller, J. K. (2010). Surveillance of selected post-caesarean infections based on electronic registries: validation study including post-discharge infections. *Journal of Hospital Infection*, 75(3), 200-204.

46. InacioMS, M. C., PaxtonMA, E. W., ChenBS, Y., HarrisRD, J., EckRN, E., Sue BarnesRN, B. S. N., ... & AkePhD, C. F. (2011). Leveraging electronic medical records for surveillance of surgical site infection in a total joint replacement population. *Infection Control and Hospital Epidemiology*, 32(4), 351-359.

47. Thompson, K., Dokholyan, R. S., Horan, T. C., Gaynes, R. P., Solomon, S. L.,

Platt, R., ... & Sands, K. E. F. (2002). Using automated health plan data to assess infection risk from coronary artery bypass surgery. *Emerging Infectious Diseases*, *8*, 1433-41.

48. Wright, S. B., Huskins, W. C., Dokholyan, R. S., Goldmann, D. A., & Platt, R. (2003). Administrative databases provide inaccurate data for surveillance of long-term central venous catheter-associated infections. *Infection Control and Hospital Epidemiology*, *24*(12), 946-949.

49. Voit, S. B., Todd, J. K., Nelson, B., & Nyquist, A. C. (2005). Electronic surveillance system for monitoring surgical antimicrobial prophylaxis. *Pediatrics*, *116*(6), 1317-1322.

50. Sands, K., Vineyard, G., Livingston, J., Christiansen, C., & Platt, R. (1999). Efficient identification of postdischarge surgical site infections: use of automated pharmacy dispensing information, administrative data, and medical record information. *Journal of Infectious Diseases*, *179*(2), 434-441.

51. Koller, W., Blacky, A., Bauer, C., Mandl, H., & Adlassnig, K. P. (2010). Electronic surveillance of healthcare-associated infections with MONI-ICU–a clinical breakthrough compared to conventional surveillance systems. *Stud Health Technol Inform*, *160*(Pt 1), 432-6.

52. Bouzbid, S., Gicquel, Q., Gerbier, S., Chomarat, M., Pradat, E., Fabry, J., ... & Metzger, M. H. (2011). Automated detection of nosocomial infections: evaluation of different strategies in an intensive care unit 2000–2006. *Journal of Hospital Infection*, *79*(1), 38-43.

53. Choudhuri, J. A., Pergamit, R. F., Chan, J. D., Schreuder, A. B., McNamara, E., Lynch, J. B., & Dellit, T. H. (2011). An electronic catheter-associated urinary tract infection surveillance tool. *Infection Control and Hospital Epidemiology*, *32*(8), 757-762.

54. Graham III, P. L., San Gabriel, P., Lutwick, S., Haas, J., & Saiman, L. (2004). Validation of a multicenter computer-based surveillance system for hospital-acquired bloodstream infections in neonatal intensive care departments. *American journal of infection control*, *32*(4), 232-234.

55. Trick, W. E., Zagorski, B. M., Tokars, J. I., Vernon, M. O., Welbel, S. F.,

Wisniewski, M. F., ... & Weinstein, R. A. (2004). Computer algorithms to detect bloodstream infections. *Emerging Infectious Diseases, 10*(9), 1612–20.

56. Woeltje, K. F., Butler, A. M., Goris, A. J., Tutlam, N. T., Doherty, J. A., M Brandon Westover, M. D., ... & Bailey, T. C. (2008). Automated surveillance for central line–associated bloodstream infection in intensive care units. *Infection Control and Hospital Epidemiology, 29*(9), 842-846.

57. Bellini, C., Petignat, C., Francioli, P., Wenger, A., Bille, J., Klopotov, A., ... & Zanetti, G. (2007). Comparison of automated strategies for surveillance of nosocomial bacteremia. *Infection Control and Hospital Epidemiology, 28*(9), 1030-1035.

58. Mendonça, E. A., Haas, J., Shagina, L., Larson, E., & Friedman, C. (2005). Extracting information on pneumonia in infants using natural language processing of radiology reports. *Journal of Biomedical Informatics, 38*(4), 314-321.

59. Klompas, M., Kleinman, K., & Platt, R. (2008). Development of an algorithm for surveillance of ventilator - associated pneumonia with electronic data and comparison of algorithm results with clinician diagnoses. *Infection Control and Hospital Epidemiology, 29*(1), 31-37.

60. Claridge, J. A., Golob Jr, J. F., Fadlalla, A. M., D'Amico, B. M., Peerless, J. R., Yowler, C. J., & Malangoni, M. A. (2009). Who Is Monitoring Your Infections: Shouldn't You Be?*. *Surgical Infections, 10*(1), 59-64.

61. Haas, J. P., Mendonça, E. A., Ross, B., Friedman, C., & Larson, E. (2005). Use of computerized surveillance to detect nosocomial pneumonia in neonatal intensive care unit patients. *American Journal of Infection Control, 33*(8), 439-443.

62. Shaklee, J., Zerr, D. M., Elward, A., Newland, J., Leckerman, K., Asti, L., ... & Zaoutis, T. (2011). Improving surveillance for pediatric Clostridium difficile infection: derivation and validation of an accurate case-finding tool. *The Pediatric Infectious Disease Journal, 30*(3), e38-e40.

63. Van Mourik, M. S., Groenwold, R. H., van der Sprenkel, J. W. B., van Solinge, W. W., Troelstra, A., & Bonten, M. J. (2011). Automated detection of external

ventricular and lumbar drain-related meningitis using laboratory and microbiology results and medication data. *PLOS ONE, 6*(8), e22846.

64. Broderick, A., Mori, M., NETTLEMAN, M. D., STREED, S. A., & Wenzel, R. P. (1990). Nosocomial infections: validation of surveillance and computer modeling to identify pat at risk. *American Journal of Epidemiology, 131*(4), 734-742.

65. Scott Evans, R., Burke, J. P., Classen, D. C., Gardner, R. M., Menlove, R. L., Goodrich, K. M., ... & Pestotnik, S. L. (1992). Computerized identification of patients at high risk for hospital-acquired infection. *American Journal of Infection Control, 20*(1), 4-10.

66. Hacek, D. M., Cordell, R. L., Noskin, G. A., & Peterson, L. R. (2004). Computer-assisted surveillance for detecting clonal outbreaks of nosocomial infection. *Journal of Clinical Microbiology, 42*(3), 1170-1175.

67. Wright, M. O., Perencevich, E. N., Novak, C., Hebden, J. N., Standiford, H. C., & Harris, A. D. (2004). Preliminary assessment of an automated surveillance system for infection control. *Infection Control and Hospital Epidemiology, 25*(4), 325-332.

68. Chang, Y. J., Yeh, M. L., Li, Y. C., Hsu, C. Y., Lin, C. C., Hsu, M. S., & Chiu, W. T. (2011). Predicting hospital-acquired infections by scoring system with simple parameters. *PLOS ONE, 6*(8), e23137.

69. Hirschhorn, L. R., Currier, J. S., & Platt, R. (1993). Electronic surveillance of antibiotic exposure and coded discharge diagnoses as indicators of postoperative infection and other quality assurance measures. *Infection Control and Hospital Epidemiology*, 21-28.

70. Baker, C., Luce, J., Chenoweth, C., & Friedman, C. (1995). Comparison of case-finding methodologies for endometritis after cesarean section. *American Journal of Infection Control, 23*(1), 27-33.

71. L Pokorny, P. T., A Rovira, M. D., Martín-Baranera, M., C Gimeno, M. D., Alonso-Tarrés, C., & Vilarasau, J. (2006). Automatic detection of patients with nosocomial infection by a computer-based surveillance system: a validation

study in a general hospital. *Infection Control and Hospital Epidemiology*, *27*(5), 500-503.

72. Evans, R. S., Gardner, R. M., Bush, A. R., Burke, J. P., Jacobson, J. A., Larsen, R. A., ... & Warner, H. R. (1985). Development of a computerized infectious disease monitor (CIDM). *Computers and Biomedical Research*, *18*(2), 103-113.

73. Infection Control Today. *Automated Surveillance: Can it Replace "Shoe-Leather" Epidemiology?*. Retrieved from http://www.theradoc.com/wp-content/uploads/2009/07/infection_control_today_Aug_2009.pdf (accessed 25 May 2013).

74. Worth, A. P., & Cronin, M. T. (2003). The use of discriminant analysis, logistic regression and classification tree analysis in the development of classification models for human health effects. *Journal of Molecular Structure: THEOCHEM*, *622*(1), 97-111.

75. The Infection Control Society of Taiwan. Retrieved from http://www.nics.org.tw/hospital_eligible.php

76. Harel, D. (1987). Statecharts: A visual formalism for complex systems. *Science of Computer Programming*, *8*(3), 231-274.

77. Centers for Disease Control of Taiwan. Retrieved from https://tnis.cdc.gov.tw/ (accessed 2 Mar 2014)

78. Adobe. *Flex overview*. Retrieved from http://www.adobe.com/products/flex.html?promoid=DINEZ (accessed 25 Aug 2013).

79. Evans, R. S., Pestotnik, S. L., Classen, D. C., Clemmer, T. P., Weaver, L. K., Orme Jr, J. F., ... & Burke, J. P. (1998). A computer-assisted management program for antibiotics and other antiinfective agents. *New England Journal of Medicine*, *338*(4), 232-238.

80. Brusaferro, S., Regattin, L., Faruzzo, A., Grasso, A., Basile, M., Calligaris, L., ... & Viale, P. (2006). Surveillance of hospital-acquired infections: a model for settings with resource constraints. *American Journal of Infection Control*, *34*(6), 362-366.

Appendix

The list of electronic hospital-associated infection surveillance information systems

Article (year)	Study setting and size	HAI types	Data sources	Data description	Sensitivity [PPV] (%)	Specificity [NPV] (%)
Bellini *et al*	University hospital, 669 episodes	BSI, CRI	Microbiology culture test results	Positive blood and CVC cultures	89.7	83.9
Bouam *et al*	Tertiary care hospital, 548 cases	BSI, UTI, CRI	Microbiology culture test results	Positive blood, urine or CVC cultures	91 [88]	91
Broderick *et al*[64]	Acute care hospital, 953 patients	Nosocomial infection	Microbiology culture test results	Positive urine and/or wound cultures	80.7 [75.3]	97.5
Brossette *et al*	Community and tertiary care hospitals, 907 patients	UTI, BSI, RTI,CDI, PWI	Microbiology culture test results	Positive blood, urine, sputum and wound cultures, serology, molecular tests	86	98.4
Chalfine *et al*	Tertiary care hospital, 766 patients	SSI	Microbiology culture test results	Positive cultures	84.3	99.9
Choudhuri *et al*	University affiliated urban teaching hospital, 136 patients	Catheter-associated UTI	Microbiology culture test results; biochemistry results; clinical patient data	Positive cultures; presence of fever and urinary tracts; abnormal leukocyte count	86.4 [85]	93.8 [94.4]
Evans *et al*	Tertiary care teaching hospital, 11280 patients	Nosocomial infection	Microbiology culture test results	Positive cultures	63 [21]	87
Graham *et al*	Acute care hospitals, 1656 cases	BSI	Microbiology culture test results	Positive blood cultures	79 [58]	96
Klompas *et al*	Academic hospital, 459 patients	VAP	Microbiology culture test results;	Gram stains of excretion samples;	95 [100]	--

			biochemistry results; radiology results; clinical patient data	abnormal leukocyte count; radiological signs of pneumonia; PEEP and FiO2 values; presence of fever		
Koller *et al*	Tertiary care and teaching hospital, 99 patients	UTI, BSI, CRI, pneumonia	Microbiology culture test results; biochemistry results; clinical patient data	Positive cultures; abnormal leukocyte count or CRP values; clinical data from a patient data management system	90.3 [100]	100 [95.8]
Mendonça *et al*	Acute care and community hospitals, 1688 neonates	Pneumonia	Radiology report results	Free text radiology reports	71 [7.5]	99
Haas *et al*	Tertiary care hospital, 2932 patients NICU	Pneumonia	Radiology report results	Free text radiology reports	71 [79]	99.8
Woeltje *et al*	Tertiary care academic hospital, 540 patients	CRI	Microbiology culture test results	Positive wound, urine or respiratory device cultures	94.3 [22.8]	68 [99.2]
Wright *et al*	Tertiary care teaching hospital, 75 control charts	Nosocomial Outbreaks	Microbiology culture test results	Predefined organisms	90.9 [61]	85.7
Hacek *et al*[66]	Tertiary care teaching hospital, 300 potential outbreaks	Nosocomial Outbreaks	Microbiology culture test results	Predefined organisms	2SD: 42.9 [75] MI: 57.1 [66.7]	2SD: 83.3 MI: 66.7
Bolon *et al*	HMO, 6,322 procedures	SSI	Procedure and discharge codes; pharmacy	ICD-9-CM codes; antimicrobial	86–93 [25–39]	--

			dispensing records	administration with an infection-specifi c interval		
Cadwallade r et al	Adult teaching hospital, 510 procedures	SSI	Procedure and discharge codes	ICD-9-CM codes	88 [95.6]	99.8
Chang et al[68]	Academic teaching medical center, 476 patients	Device-rel ated	Procedure and discharge codes; pharmacy dispensing records	ICD-9-CM codes; administration of steroids	92.4–96.6 [70.6–79.1]	86.0–91.5 [97.2–98.7]
Hirschhorn et al[69]	Women's teaching hospital, 2197 patients	Nosocomia l postpartum	Procedure and discharge codes; pharmacy dispensing records	ICD-9-CM codes; antibiotic exposure	59 [PPV 94]	>99
Inacio et al	HMO, 42173 procedures	SSI	Procedure and discharge codes; physician narratives	ICD-9-CM codes; standardized postoperative forms	97.8 [11]	91.5 [100]
Moro and Morsillo	HMO, 6158 patients	SSI	Procedure and discharge codes	ICD-9-CM codes	20.6	99.1
Sands et al	HMO, 3,636 patients	CVC-relate d SSI	Procedure and discharge codes; pharmacy dispensing records	ICD-9-CM codes; antimicrobial exposure; claims records	74 [48]	98
Shaklee et al	Pediatric hospitals, 119 patients	CDI	Procedure and discharge codes	ICD-9-CM codes	80.7 [73.95]	99.9 [99.9]
Sherman et al	Academic tertiary care pediatric hospital, 1072 cases	CRI, VAP, SSI	Procedure and discharge codes	ICD-9-CM codes	61 [20]	96 [99]
Yokoe et al	HMO, 22313 procedures	SSI	Procedure and discharge codes;	ICD-9-CM codes;	93–97 [33–38]	–

			pharmacy dispensing records	infection-specific antimicrobial exposure		
Yokoe *et al* (2001)	HMO, 2746 female patients	CVC-related SSI, UTI, PWI	Procedure and discharge codes; pharmacy dispensing records	ICD-9-CM codes; COSTAR codes; antimicrobial exposure	96 [40]	99
Baker *et al*[70]	Tertiary care teaching hospital, 167 women	Nosocomial endometritis	Procedure and discharge codes; pharmacy dispensing records	ICD-9-CM codes; postoperative antibiotics	89 [53]	95
Platt *et al*	HMO, 1953 patients	SSI	Procedure and discharge codes; pharmacy dispensing records	ICD-9-CM codes; antimicrobial exposure; claims records, CPT codes	[53]	--
Wright and Huskins *et al*	HMO, 8483 patients	CVC-related SSI	Procedure and discharge codes	ICD-9-CM codes; CPT codes; COSTAR codes; claims records	[86]	--
Bouzbid *et al*	University hospital, 1499 patients	UTI, BSI, CRI, pneumonia	System 1: physician narratives System 2: pharmacy dispensing records; microbiology culture test results	Electronic discharge summaries; ATC codes for antimicrobial administration; positive cultures of non-common skin contaminants	System 1: 86.7 System 2: 99.3 [34.7]	System 1: 88.2 System 2: 56.8 [99.7]
Claridge *et al*	Level I trauma center, 769 patients	VAP	Pharmacy dispensing records; microbiology culture test results; clinical patient data	Antimicrobial treatment records; positive cultures; vital signs; presence of devices	97 [100]	100 [99.9]

Leth *et al*	Community hospitals, 1512 women	SSI, UTI	Procedure and discharge codes; pharmacy dispensing records; microbiology culture test results	ICD-10 and NCSP codes; ATC codes for antimicrobial administration; positive urine or wound cultures	74 [81.7]	99.4 [99.3]
Leth and Møller	Single hospital, 1129 patients	UTI, BSI, Pneumonia, PWI	Pharmacy dispensing records; microbiology laboratory results; biochemistry results	Antimicrobial exposure; positive blood, urine, wound and drainage cultures; abnormal leukocyte counts and CRP values	94 [21]	47 [98]
Pokorny *et al*[71]	Acute care teaching hospital, 1043 patients	Nosocomial infection	Procedure and discharge codes; pharmacy dispensing records; microbiology culture test results	ICD-9-CM codes; antimicrobial exposure; positive cultures	94.3 [55.9]	83.6 [98.5]
Spolaore *et al*	Acute care hospitals, 865 cases	SSI	Procedure and discharge codes; microbiology culture test results	ICD-9-CM codes; positive wound and drainage cultures	[97]	--
Trick *et al*	Teaching and community hospitals, 127 patients	CRI	Microbiology culture test results; pharmacy dispensing records	Positive blood or wound cultures; vancomycin exposure interval	81 [62]	72 [87]
van Mourik *et al*	Tertiary healthcare centre, 537 patients	Drain-related meningitis	Pharmacy dispensing records; microbiology laboratory	Number and exposure time of antimicrobial drugs; positive cerebrospinal	98.8 [56.9]	87.9 [99.9]

			results; biochemistry results	fluid and drain cultures; abnormal leukocyte and CRP values		
Voit *et al*	Paediatric hospitals, 1493 patients	SSI	ICD-9-CM codes; pharmacy dispensing records; microbiology laboratory results	ICD-9-CM surgical procedure codes; administration and duration of antibiotics; microbiological laboratory data	--	90
Lo *et al*	Tertiary-care teaching hospital, 11251 patients	UTI	Pharmacy dispensing records; microbiology laboratory results; biochemistry results; procedure codes; clinical patient data	Positive blood and urine cultures; routine urinalysis results; invasive devices; fever records	100	94.61

CDI, Clostridium difficile-related infection; COSTAR, computerized stored ambulatory records; CRI, CVC-related infection; CRP, C reactive protein; CVC, central venous catheter; HMO, health maintenance organization; ICD-9-CM, International Classification of Diseases 9th revision, clinical modification; NPV, negative predictive value; PPV, positive predictive value; PWI, postoperative wound infection; RTI, respiratory tract infection; VAP, ventilator-associated pneumonia; ATC, Anatomical Therapeutic Chemical; NCSP, NOMESCO Classification of Surgical Procedures; PEEP, positive end-expiratory pressure

Printed by Books on Demand GmbH, Norderstedt / Germany